True Survival

APOLLO 13

MISSION TO THE MOON

Virginia Loh-Hagan

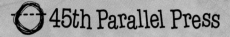

45th Parallel Press

Published in the United States of America by Cherry Lake Publishing
Ann Arbor, Michigan
www.cherrylakepublishing.com

Reading Adviser: Marla Conn MS, Ed., Literacy specialist, Read-Ability, Inc.
Book Designer: Felicia Macheske

Photo Credits: © NASA, cover, 5, 7, 8, 11, 21, 22, 27, 29; © alexkoral/Shutterstock.com, cover; © mike mols/Shutterstock.com, 12; © Vladi333/Shutterstock.com, 15; © Paul_Brighton/Shutterstock.com, 17; © ESB Professional/Shutterstock.com, 18; © Gorodenkoff/Shutterstock.com, 24

Graphic Elements Throughout: © Gordan/Shutterstock.com; © adike/Shutterstock.com; © Yure/Shutterstock.com

45th Parallel Press is an imprint of Cherry Lake Publishing.

Library of Congress Cataloging-in-Publication Data

Names: Loh-Hagan, Virginia, author.
Title: Apollo 13 : mission to the moon / by Virginia Loh-Hagan.
Description: Ann Arbor : Cherry Lake Publishing, [2018] | Series: True survival | Includes bibliographical references and index. | Audience: Grades 4 to 6.
Identifiers: LCCN 2017029639| ISBN 9781534107724 (hardcover) | ISBN 9781534109704 (PDF) | ISBN 9781534108714 (pbk.) | ISBN 9781534120693 (hosted eBook)
Subjects: LCSH: Space vehicle accidents—United States—Juvenile literature. | Apollo 13 (Spacecraft)—Accidents—Juvenile literature. | Space flight to the moon—Juvenile literature.
Classification: LCC TL789.8.U6 A5485 2018 | DDC 629.45/4—dc23
LC record available at https://lccn.loc.gov/2017029639

Cherry Lake Publishing would like to acknowledge the work of The Partnership for 21st Century Skills. Please visit *www.p21.org* for more information.

Printed in the United States of America
Corporate Graphics

table of contents

chapter one

Moonwalking

What are the three Apollo missions? Why did people think *Apollo 13* was unlucky?

Neil Armstrong and Buzz Aldrin were the first two humans on the moon. They were on *Apollo 11*. This was the first **manned** moon landing mission. Manned means flown by a human. This happened on July 20, 1969.

Armstrong took the first step on the moon. He said, "That's one small step for man, one giant leap for mankind." *Apollo 11* paved the way for more moon **missions**. Missions are trips with goals.

Apollo 12 launched on November 14, 1969. It flew higher than *Apollo 11*. Its goal was to study the moon. It practiced **precision** landing. Precision means being exact.

Armstrong and Aldrin spent a day on the moon.

spotlight biography

Katherine Johnson was born in West Virginia. She was born in 1918. She loved counting. She counted everything. Her neighborhood schools wouldn't let her in. It was because she was black and female. That didn't stop her. She finished college at age 18. She went to graduate school. She was one of three black students. She was the only woman. She got hired by NASA. She was a "human computer." She did hard math problems. Her math sent people to the moon and back. She figured out flight paths. She figured out how to get space shuttles to go around Earth. She wasn't treated fairly. She wasn't allowed to put her name on reports. She did anyway. She wasn't allowed to go to meetings. She did anyway. She took giant steps for women and blacks.

Apollo 13 was to be the third mission to the moon. Its goal was to bring back moon pieces. There were three **astronauts**. Astronauts are people who fly into space. They do everything. They're the **crew**. The crew is made of people who work in the shuttle. The commander was James A. Lovell Jr. The other pilots were John L. Swigert Jr. and Fred W. Haise Jr.

Lovell was the world's most traveled astronaut. He had a lot of space experience. He had 572 hours of space flight. He had already done three missions.

Astronauts get a lot of training.

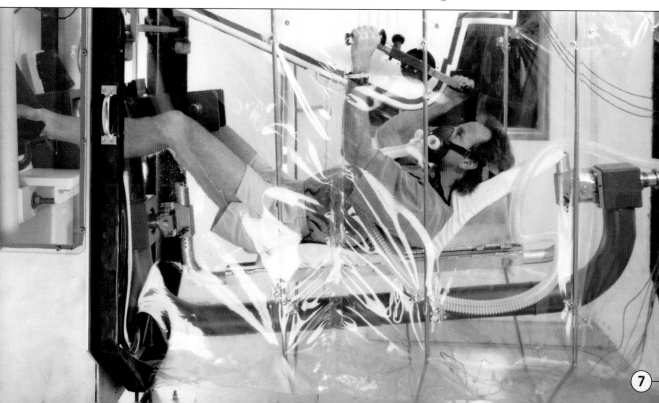

Apollo 13 had two different **units**. A unit is a single thing that is a part of something larger. A tunnel connected them. One unit was the *Odyssey*. It was used for **orbiting**. Orbit means to go around. The other unit was *Aquarius*. It was used for landing on the moon. The crew would live in the *Odyssey*.

Apollo 13 launched from Cape Canaveral, Florida. It lifted off on April 11, 1970. It was on a path to the moon. People were worried. They thought the number 13 was unlucky. They thought *Apollo 13* would be unlucky. Also, the launch time was 1:13 p.m. This is 13:13 in military time.

Things went well at first. Then, on April 13, the crew heard a loud bang.

◄ Liftoff is another word for launch.

chapter two

Mayday!

What happened to *Apollo 13*? What does "Houston" mean?

One of the **oxygen** tanks exploded. Oxygen is the air we breathe. There is no oxygen in space. Astronauts needed the oxygen in the tanks. This happened during the flight. This blew out a part of the shuttle. It caused damage. *Odyssey* lost power, light, and water. The crew was about 200,000 miles (321,869 kilometers) from Earth.

Swigert and Lovell called **mission control**. Mission control manages space flights. Swigert and Lovell said, "Houston, we've had a problem."

Houston is in Texas. It's the base for space flight activities. It's the home of **NASA**'s space center. NASA stands for the National Aeronautics and Space Administration. This organization is in charge of space travel.

Apollo 13 was in flight for more than 50 hours before the mission was aborted.

The crew got worried. They didn't have enough power to go to the moon. They didn't have enough power to get home. They could get stuck in space.

Oxygen leaked out. The crew was losing air. They couldn't breathe. Bad gases were building up. This could kill them.

Apollo 13 **aborted** its mission. Abort means to stop. The crew couldn't land on the moon. They had to go around it. They had to return to Earth. *Apollo 13* had a new mission. The mission was to get home safely. Everyone was worried about the astronauts.

Many people watched the events on TV or listened on the radio.

explained by science

Space shuttles send astronauts to and from space. They have three main parts: rocket boosters, gas tank, and orbiter. The two rocket boosters lift the shuttle off the ground. They blast the shuttle into space. The tank is on the outside of the shuttle. It holds gas. An orbiter carries people and things. Space shuttles are rockets. They aren't engines. Engines need air. Rockets don't need air to run. Space doesn't have air. Gas launches the space shuttle up and out. The gas tank falls off. This lets the shuttle orbit at a lighter weight. In space, the shuttle uses Earth's natural pull to stay in orbit.

chapter three

Surviving in Space

**What did the astronauts do in space?
How did they survive?**

The astronauts were four days away from Earth. *Odyssey* was operating on emergency battery power. But they needed to save that power. They needed the *Odyssey* to get back to Earth. So they shut it off. The *Aquarius* was off, so they powered it up.

Aquarius would explode during **reentry** because it didn't have a heat shield. Reentry is when shuttles return to Earth. The **atmosphere** surrounds Earth. It's a layer of gases. Most things burn up when they pass the atmosphere. Shuttles must pass through and not burn up. They must stay cool. They must stay in one piece. They must return to the ground.

Reentry is the hardest part of space travel.

would you?

- **Would you go to space?** Space is exciting. But there are risks. You'd die quickly without a spacesuit. You wouldn't be able to breathe. You could get hit by space rocks.

- **Would you spend money to go to Mars?** One company guesses it would cost $6 billion to send the first four people to Mars. This includes the shuttle, training, and gear. There's a lot that goes into space travel.

- **Would you use the bathroom in space?** Astronauts used to pee and poop in a bag. Today, astronauts have to go to space toilet training. They use special toilets. These toilets pull waste away from the body. They're like a hose with a vacuum. They cost millions of dollars.

The crew was 20 hours from the moon. But they no longer focused on a moon landing. They focused on surviving. They moved into *Aquarius*. They used it like a lifeboat. They lived in it. They waited to get closer to Earth. Then, they'd move into the *Odyssey*.

Aquarius was a smaller area. It didn't have enough food. It only had food for 2 days for 2 men. There were 3 of them. The crew had to make it last. They had to save **resources**. Resources are things needed in order to live.

The crew drank fruit juices. They ate hot dogs.

Water was the main worry. The crew didn't have enough water. They would run out. This would happen 5 hours before hitting Earth. The crew saved water. They cut down to 6 ounces (177 milliliters) each per day. Their bodies lost water.

Electrical systems were turned off. This was to save power. This meant there was no heat. Water formed on the walls. It was really cold. The crew was freezing. They had a hard time sleeping.

◀ People have nightmares about being trapped in space.

chapter four

Mission Control to the Rescue!

How did *Apollo 13* get rescued? Why was mission control important? Where did *Apollo 13* land?

Mission control had teams of experts. These experts worked hard. They figured out problems. They hadn't prepared for this emergency. They had to work fast. They created new plans. They came up with new ideas. They helped the crew. They talked to the crew over the radio.

They practiced different ways to help the crew. They created **simulations**. Simulations are copies of the real thing. The experts pretended like they were in the shuttle. They tested ideas. When things worked, they told the crew. For example, they helped with the bad gases. They made an air cleaner. They used things available on the shuttle. They told the crew how to make this.

The crew lost radio control when they swung around the moon.

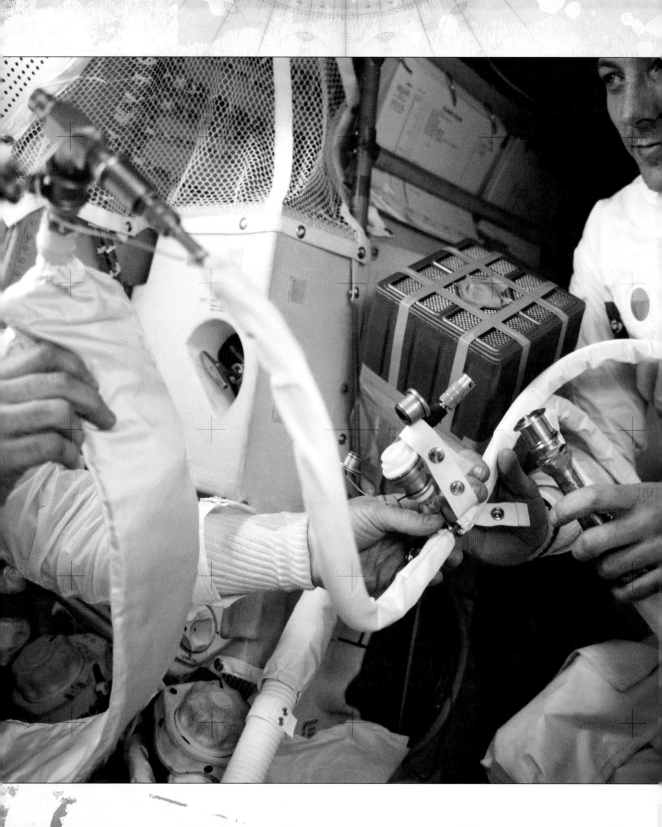

The experts figured out how to get the crew home. They needed to do this quickly. They did a lot of math. They came up with a plan.

They told the crew to move into the *Odyssey*. The crew powered it back up. This was a problem. Powering up in flight had never been done before. There was also water on the machines. This could cause a breakdown. Mission control figured out how to make it work.

The crew needed to let go of the *Aquarius*. The shuttles needed to be a safe distance apart. But there wasn't enough power to push the *Aquarius* off. Mission control did the math. They figured out the right amount of pressure that wouldn't waste power but would keep the astronauts safe.

◄ Mission control took 3 days to do what normally would take 3 months.

Computers are important for space travel.

Apollo 13 entered Earth's atmosphere. There was a radio **blackout**. Radio blackouts are silence. There was no contact. This lasted 6 minutes. This was 87 seconds longer than expected. People thought the shuttle had exploded. They were scared. They were worried.

Then, there was contact. Mission control heard from the crew. *Apollo 13* hit its target. It landed in the Pacific Ocean. It landed south of Samoa. Samoa is an island. *Apollo 13* landed on April 17. They landed at 1:07 p.m. It was a safe return.

World leaders helped. They sent ships to the rescue area. Everyone was happy. The astronauts were finally home!

survival tips

TRAPPED IN SPACE!

- Wear a spacesuit. Spacesuits trap air that lets people breathe. They also protect people from the sun's rays, heat, and cold.

- Find a comet. Comets are bits of ice and rock. They travel toward the sun. Top layers fall off. Ice is locked inside. It melts. Some people think this is water you can drink.

- Be open to change. Some scientists think life changes over billions of years. Life changes to match the environment.

- Be smart with your stuff. You can only use what you bring with you. You can't get more stuff. You can't get rid of stuff. You have to reuse your things.

chapter five

Back on Earth

What happened to the crew after they landed? What did the investigation reveal? Why is *Apollo 13* important?

The crew survived. They were in good shape except for Haise. Haise got sick. He didn't have enough water. But he got better. They all became heroes.

There was an **investigation**. Investigation means people were trying to figure out what happened. It was done by the *Apollo 13* Review Board. It took 2 months. People wanted to know what went wrong with *Apollo 13*. A heating wire was inside the oxygen tank. It lost its covering. This caused it to explode. The Review Board also found other mistakes. NASA used this information. It created safer shuttles. It created better actions.

Splashdown is when a spacecraft returns to earth by landing in the ocean.

Rest in Peace

Christa McAuliffe was born in 1948. She was a high school teacher. She taught American history and English. In 1984, President Reagan and NASA started the Teacher in Space Program. They wanted a teacher who could teach students while in space. McAuliffe dreamed of going to space. She applied. Over 11,000 people applied. She got picked. Vice President George H. W. Bush said she was the "first private citizen passenger in the history of space flight." She trained for a year. On January 28, 1986, she boarded the *Challenger*. Six other people went. Her shuttle exploded. McAuliffe died. She was an extraordinary teacher. She wanted students to learn about space. She will be remembered.

The Apollo 13 mission was called "a successful failure." The crew failed to land on the moon. But they returned home safely. Mission control learned a lot. They learned how to rescue a crew. They saved lives without having a plan in advance. They made plans as things happened. The mission also reminded everyone of the dangers of space flight.

Apollo 13 did achieve some goals. The crew took 11 pictures of Earth. They passed the far side of the moon and set a record. This mission was the farthest humans had ever traveled from Earth.

Astronauts are welcomed home as heroes.

Did You Know?

- A famous saying is "Houston, we have a problem." This is wrong. It's a historical misquote. Misquote means to not say something correctly.

- John Swigert said, "Okay Houston, we've had a problem here." Mission control couldn't hear him. Jim Lovell repeated the line. He said, "Ahh, Houston, we've had a problem." Mission control heard Lovell. So, Lovell got credit for saying the line.

- *Apollo 17* was the last manned moon mission. It happened in 1972.

- Charles Duke was a backup astronaut. He exposed Ken Mattingly to measles. He didn't mean to do it. Mattingly was supposed to fly in *Apollo 13*. NASA was scared he'd get sick. So, they replaced him. John Swigert went instead. Mattingly never got the measles.

- The first 2 days of the *Apollo 13* flight went well. Joe Kerwin worked at mission control. He said, "The spacecraft is in real good shape as far as we are concerned. We're bored to tears down here." Soon after, no one complained of boredom.

- In 1995, a movie called *Apollo 13* was made. Tom Hanks is an actor. He played Lovell in the movie. Hanks has an asteroid named for him. The asteroid is called "12818 Tomhanks (1996 GU8)."

- Astronauts said the moon smells bad. They got moondust on their spacesuits. The moondust smells like spent gunpowder. Some astronauts got moondust in their mouths.

Consider This!

Take a Position: Going to space costs a lot of money. It can also be dangerous. Do you think the United States should continue the space program? Is it important for us to be in space? Argue your point with reasons and evidence.

Say What? Learn more about the International Space Station. Do research. Explain what it is. Explain who is involved. Explain what it does.

Think About It! Read more about *Apollo 13*. Then, watch the movie *Apollo 13*. How is the film true to what happened in history? How is it different? (Most moviemakers change history to make the story more interesting.)

Learn More

- Graham, Ian. *You Wouldn't Want to Be on Apollo 13*. New York: Franklin Watts, 2017.

- Holden, Henry M. *Danger in Space: Surviving the Apollo 13 Disaster*. Berkeley Heights, NJ: Enslow Publishers, 2013.

- Radomski, Kassandra. *The Apollo 13 Mission: Core Events of a Crisis in Space*. North Mankato, MN: Capstone Press, 2014.

Glossary

aborted (uh-BORT-id) stopped

astronauts (AS-truh-nawts) people who fly to space

atmosphere (AT-muhs-feer) layer of gases around Earth

blackout (BLAK-out) silence

crew (KROO) the members of a flight, the workers

investigation (in-ves-tih-GAY-shuhn) research, an examination

manned (MAND) flown by a human

mission control (MISH-uhn kuhn-TROHL) the experts who help manage a space flight

missions (MISH-uhnz) journeys or trips with specific goals

NASA (NAS-uh) National Aeronautics and Space Administration

orbiting (OR-bit-ing) the act of going around

oxygen (AHK-sih-juhn) the air we breathe

precision (prih-SIZH-uhn) being exact or accurate

reentry (ree-EN-tree) the act of returning to Earth through its atmosphere

resources (REE-sors-iz) things needed to survive, like water and food

simulations (sim-yuh-LAY-shuhnz) the act of copying the real thing

units (YOO-nihtz) single things that are a part of something larger

Index

About the Author

Dr. Virginia Loh-Hagan is an author, university professor, former classroom teacher, and curriculum designer. Her first draft of this book consisted of 1,313 words. (She did not do this on purpose.) She lives in San Diego with her very tall husband and very naughty dogs. To learn more about her, visit www.virginialoh.com.